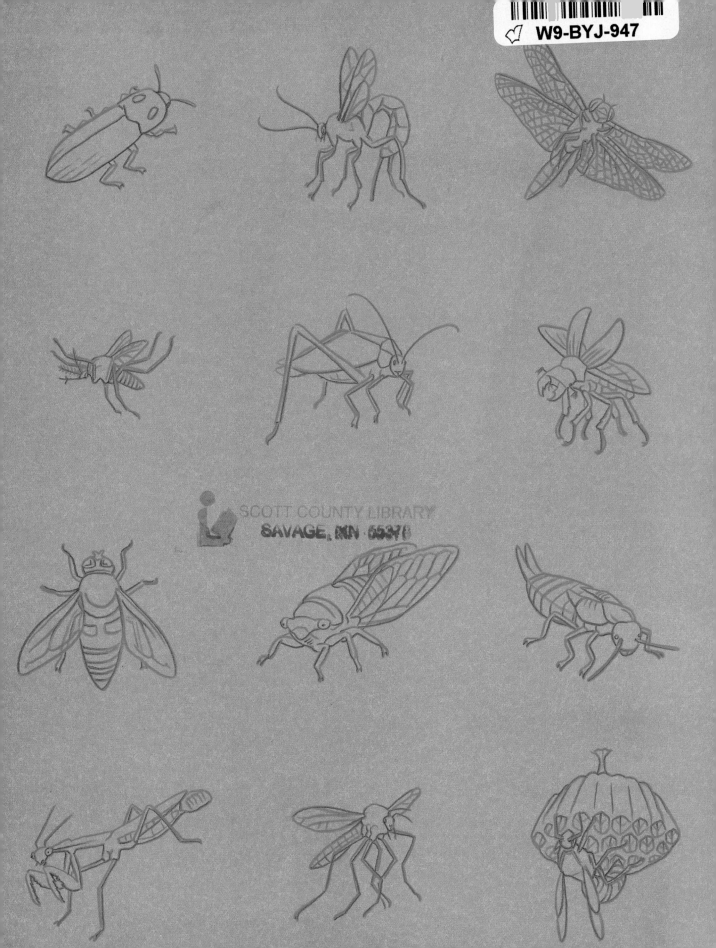

Will You Sting Me?
Will You Bite?

The Truth About Some Scary-Looking Insects

by Sara Swan Miller

Illustrations by
Rick Chrustowski

Stemmer House

PUBLISHERS

Inquiries should be directed to
Stemmer House Publishers, Inc.
2627 Caves Road
Owings Mills, Maryland 21117
U.S.A.

A Barbara Holdridge book

Printed in China
First Edition

          Library of Congress Cataloging-in-Publication Data
Miller, Sara Swan.
   Will you sting me? Will you bite? : the truth about some scary-looking insects / by Sara
Swan Miller ; illustrations by Rick Chrustowski.
      p. cm. -- (The curious little critters series)
   ISBN 0-88045-144-0 -- ISBN 0-88045-145-9 (pbk.)
      1. Insects--Juvenile literature. 2. Insect pests--Juvenile literature. 3. Bites and
stings--Juvenile literature. [1. Insects. 2. Insect pests. 3. Bites and stings.] I. Chrustowski,
Rick, ill. II. Title.
QL467.2 .M545 2001
595.7--dc21   2001020896

Designed by Barbara Holdridge
Layout in Caslon Old Face and ITC Caslon 224 with prepress by Hellen Hom
Printed on 106 pound acid-free paper and
bound by Regent Publishing Services, Hong Kong

For Ilka.
Share it with your grandchildren!
S.S.M.

For Mom and Dad with love.
P.S. Happy Bug Day!
R.C.

Contents

DRAGONFLY

Here comes a big, scary-looking insect! Its eyes are like huge goggles. Its tail is long and pointed. It swoops down and flies right at you! Will it sting?

In the old days people called dragonflies "darning needles." They thought one would fly down and sew up their ears.

But the dragonfly doesn't care about your ears. Or your nose. It doesn't care about you at all. And it can't sting.

All it wants to do is catch a flying insect to eat. It has a bunch of spiny legs right under its mouth. They look like a basket. It swoops after an insect and catches it in its basket. Then it pops its lunch into its mouth.

Its big eyes are made up of lots and lots of tiny eyes. It can look up and down and sideways all at once. Try to catch one. Zip! It flies away.

A baby dragonfly lives on the bottom of a pond. It is brown and wide and funny-looking. It eats insects, too. It eats and eats. Soon it grows too big for its skin and climbs out. Then it grows some more. It keeps shedding its old skins.

One day it crawls out of the water and hangs onto a tree. Its skin splits open for the last time. Out climbs a beautiful dragonfly. It stretches its wings and flies away.

Do you know what a dragonfly's favorite food is? Mosquitoes! Be glad there are lots of dragonflies to eat them up!

The Dragonfly

The dragonfly is not so scary–
Has she any sharp teeth?
Are her nostrils hairy?
You may even find
That she's someone you like
'Cause she gobbles mosquitoes
And others that bite.

But long ago
When the world was new
Before there were "dinos"
And long before YOU,
The dragonfly got as big as a cat!
Now, how would you like to meet up with *that*?

10

PAPER WASP

Here's a funny-looking thing! It looks like a small round waffle. It hangs upside down from a stem. It's made of gray paper.

Be careful! This is a paper wasp's nest. The mother wasp is coming! She's afraid you will hurt her babies. If you touch the nest, she will sting you!

But it's safe to look at it. Just don't come too close. Stay at least ten feet away to be safe. How did the mother wasp make it? She chewed up pieces of sticks and wooden clothespins. She mixed the chewed wood with her spit. Then she used her front legs to make each six-sided room. She laid an egg in each room. The babies that hatch look like small white worms.

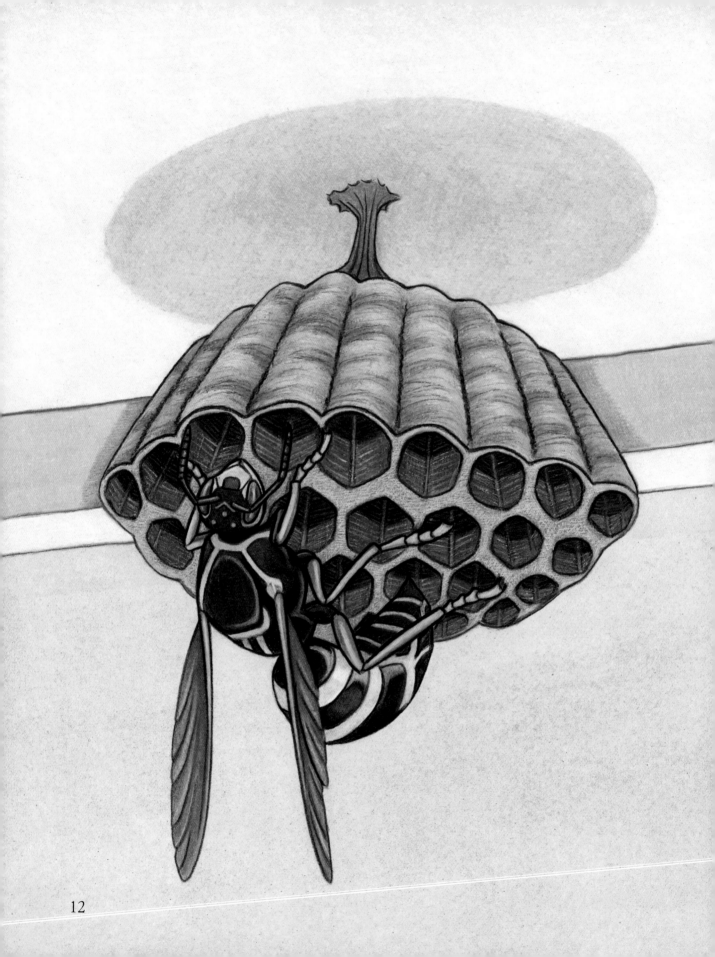

The mother wasp flies back and forth feeding her babies. She catches an insect and chews it up. Then she pushes it into a baby wasp's face. Baby eats it right up. Yum!

Finally, the babies grow big and fat. Now they rest in their rooms, not eating. As they rest, they change into grown-up wasps.

Most of the adult wasps are workers. They help their mother take care of the other babies.

But some of the adult wasps just sit around on the nest. Some are males and some are females. The males have no stingers. They won't hurt anybody. You can tell them by their yellow faces. The females have black faces. And they have sharp stingers.

Finally, those males and females decide it's time to fly away and mate. Afterwards, the males die.

But the new mothers sleep in a safe place all winter. When spring comes, they get to work making their own paper nests and protecting their babies. Be careful!

Amazing Wasp

She makes her nest of paper–
I know *I* couldn't do it!
(She'll lay her eggs there later.)
She says there's nothing to it!

CRANE FLY

One night you're lying in bed, ready to go to sleep. But just before you close your eyes, you see a GIANT mosquito walking on the ceiling! Will it give you a giant, painful bite? How can you sleep with *that monster* in your room?

Relax. Go to sleep. That's no mosquito. That's just a crane fly.

A crane fly won't hurt you. It doesn't even have a biting mouth. In fact, most adult crane flies don't even eat.

Then what is it doing on your ceiling? Crane flies, like moths, fly toward lights. Usually, they fly up toward the light of the moon, looking for another crane fly to mate with. But if there's a light on in your bedroom, and your window is open, they will fly right in. One light is as good as another for a crane fly.

If you visit a pond or stream, you may see a swarm of crane flies dancing in the air. Those are the males showing off, trying to get the females to mate with them. Later, the females will lay their eggs in the water or in the mud.

The young crane flies, called larvae, don't look at all like their parents. They look like fat, legless caterpillars.

You may find a crane fly larva on the bottom of the stream. Look at it closely. Do you see a disk at the end of its tail? If you look even closer, you'll see tiny tubes around the disk. When it needs air, the larva sticks its disk up out of the water and breathes through the tubes. It's like having a snorkel.

Crane fly larvae look strange, but they won't hurt you. All they want is a nice, tasty worm to wriggle near—their favorite food!

A Giant

On the ceiling at bedtime
One warm summer night, you
Spot a GIANT mosquito!
Is it coming to bite you?

Relax. Go to sleep.
Curl up safe in your nest.
That harmless old crane fly's
Just taking a rest.

MOSQUITO

Do you hear that high whining sound? Watch out! That's a mosquito coming! And, yes, she may bite you! Everyone knows the whine of a mosquito on its way. But what you may not know is that not all mosquitoes bite. Male mosquitoes spend their days and nights sucking nectar from flowers. They never bite anybody.

A female mosquito sucks nectar, too. But every so often she needs a good meal of blood to help her eggs grow inside her. She may get her blood meal from a bird or a deer or a dog. But if you happen by, she is just as happy to choose *you* to be the blood donor!

A female mosquito's mouth is made for drawing blood. There are six sharp needles on her mouth. She uses four of them to jab into someone's skin. The other two needles join together to make a kind of straw—perfect for blood-sucking.

Later, she lays her eggs on top of a pond or puddle. The young that hatch are called "wrigglers." If you have ever seen some, you know why. They look like tiny wriggling worms hanging from the surface of the water. Don't worry. They won't bite you. They are too busy eating even tinier plants and animals.

How can you keep from getting bitten by a grown female? It doesn't help to move to another country. Mosquitoes live all over the world, even up near the North Pole. The best idea is to spray insect repellant on your clothes. Mosquitoes hate the smell! Too bad for the deer and wolves and birds in the woods, though. They haven't found insect repellant yet!

The Whiner

The mosquito is a whiny one—
She never stops complaining!
She whines through all the sunny days
And also when it's raining.

You'll hear her whining day or night.
(I think she needs a tissue!)
The only time she seems to smile
Is right before she sticks you.

ICHNEUMON
(Ick NOO Mon)

Here comes the scariest insect of all! Its body is two inches long. And its sharp tail is three inches long! Imagine if it tries to sting you! Its stinger could go right through your arm!

Don't worry. That's not a stinger at all. It's just an egg-layer.

You may see a female ichneumon crawling around on a tree trunk. Suddenly she stops crawling. She sticks her egg-layer into the tree and starts to drill. It can take her half an hour to drill all the way into the tree. Then she lays her egg inside a baby horntail way inside the tree.

Horntails are insects that live in trees. The babies eat the inside of the tree. After the babies have chewed on a tree for six years or so, the tree can die.

When the baby ichneumon hatches, it finds itself inside a baby horntail. It starts eating the horntail from inside. By the time the ichneumon has finished eating, it is grown up. Then it tunnels out of the tree and flies away.

How does the mother ichneumon know where the horntail baby is? She can't see inside the tree. So she uses her feelers. They are like her ears. She can "hear" the horntail babies chewing away inside the tree. Her feelers tell her just where to drill and lay her egg.

Thanks to the ichneumon, there are not so many horntails around to chew up the trees.

The Ichneumon's Excuse

I'll bet your mother told you,
"*Never* eat a baby!"
My mother says it's good for me,
And she's a smart old lady!

And if you didn't eat it
From nose to toes to knees,
You'd be the one who's sorry!
It would eat up all your trees!

STAG BEETLE

Look at this monster flying around your porch light! Its huge, toothed jaws are as big as its head! Surely this one wants to bite you! Why else would it have those gigantic jaws?

The stag beetle is another insect that looks a lot fiercer than it really is. Those jaws are not for biting anybody. They're for fighting with another stag beetle.

They're called "stag" beetles because their jaws look like a stag's antlers. Like male deer, male stag beetles fight each other to win a female. They lock their jaws together and push each other back and forth. Finally, one of them gives up. The other one gets to mate with the female waiting nearby.

You would think with jaws that big, stag beetles must be fierce hunters. Surprise! They don't hunt anything. The young live in old logs and stumps and eat the rotting wood. The adults mostly lap plant juices. Sometimes they sip the sweet honey-dew that little insects called aphids make. Some adult stag beetles eat nothing at all.

Some can make themselves look awfully scary, though. If you bother one of these, it will rear up and open its jaws wide. But don't let a stag beetle fool you. Even if it does bite you with its big jaws, all it can do is give you a little pinch. The stag beetle is nothing but a big bluffer!

Stag Wars

Up in the treetops
Late in the night
The "stags" are having
A terrible fight!

"*I'm* better!"
"No, *me*!"
"*I'm* stronger!"
"We'll see!"
"*I'll* win her!"
"*I* might!"
"I'll beat you!"
"You're right!"

25

KATYDID

One evening you are sitting on the porch, listening to the sounds of the night–"Katydid! Katydid! Katydid! Katydidn't!" Suddenly, something large and green comes flying through the air and lands with a THUMP on your chair. It has a great humped back and long, saw-toothed legs. A sword pokes out of its tail. Help! Will it jump on you and sting you?

No, your visitor won't hurt you. She's just a female katydid. That sword on her tail is really only an egg-layer.

Watch her for a while. Every so often she takes a slo-o-ow step with one leg. Then she takes another slo-o-ow step with another leg. It looks as if it will take forever for her to walk across the back of your chair!

What is she doing here? She's listening to the males singing in the tree–"Katydid! Katydid! Katydid! Katydidn't!" This argument goes on all night. Did she or didn't she?

Of course, the male katydids aren't really arguing. They're calling to the females. On one wing they have a ridge. On the other they have a kind of file. When they run the file back and forth over the ridge, it comes out, "Katydid!"

Can you find the female katydid's ears? They're not on her head. Look closely at her front legs. Do you see two little holes on either side of her knees? Believe it or not, those are her ears! After listening for hours, she finally makes up her mind which male sounds best. She goes off to find him and mate.

Katydids sing from late summer into the fall. But when it gets cold, the nights grow silent. You'll have to wait until next summer to enjoy their music again.

The Katydid's Ditty

"Katydid! Katydid!"
Large and green.
"Katydid! Katydid!"
Walks like a queen.

"Katydid! Katydid!"
All night through....
The only thing I want to know
Is, What did Katy *DO*?

CLICK BEETLE

What are those giant, scary eyes staring up at you from the forest floor? Do they belong to a giant, scary insect? Wait! Look again. Those aren't eyes at all. Those are just big spots on a click beetle's back.

This kind of click beetle is called an elater. Those big, eye-like spots scare away birds and other insect-eating animals, too. They think the spots really are the eyes of a big animal. They're not about to try to eat anything that big! Little do they know that the little elater is completely harmless.

The elater, like other click beetles, has another trick. If it lands on its back, it snaps its body backward. Click! It flips into the air and lands back on the ground. What if it lands on its back again? Click! It snaps up into the air. It keeps on clicking until it finally lands on its feet.

Adult click beetles are fun to watch, and they don't do anybody any harm. But the young ones don't look at all like their parents and can be a big problem. They're called wireworms because they look like thin, reddish worms.

Their favorite thing to do is eat. They love to get into your garden and chew on plant roots. Even better, they love eating the seeds you have just planted. What's worse, it can take eight years before a wireworm grows up. And all that time it's eating and eating. You can understand why farmers are not very fond of young click beetles!

The Clicker

The elater's a beetle
With a neat little trick–
If she falls on her back,
She jumps up with a CLICK!

She keeps flicking and clicking
'Til she lands on her feet.
Then she wiggles her feelers
And walks on down the street!

FLOWER FLY

Uh, oh! Is that a bee? It looks like a bee. It sounds like a bee. Does it sting like a bee?

Ha, ha! The flower fly fooled you! It fools birds, too. They are afraid to eat it. They don't want to get stung either!

But the flower fly has no stinger. It just dresses like a bee to scare you. It's kind of like wearing a monster costume on Halloween. Some flower flies look like wasps, and others look like hornets. Some look like bumblebees, and some like yellow jackets.

How can you tell it's just a flower fly in disguise? Look at its feelers. They are short and straight. A bee's feelers are long and have an "elbow" in them. The flower fly has big eyes that meet in the middle. A bee's eyes are on the sides of its head. The flower fly has just one pair of wings. Bees have two pairs.

But the flower fly won't give you much time to look. If only it would hold still! But it is always in a hurry. It keeps zipping from flower to flower.

Inside a flower is yellow powder called pollen. This is what the flower fly likes to eat. Some of the pollen sticks to its furry body. It falls off into the next flower the fly visits.

The pollen helps a flower seed to start growing in the flower. The seed will fall to the ground and grow into a new plant.

Flower flies are like gardeners. Wherever they go, they make flowers grow.

Boast of the Flower Fly

I'm mean! I'm scary!
I'm big! I'm hairy!
I sting! I stab!
I poke! I jab!
I'm bad! I'm cool!
Oh–APRIL FOOL!

EARWIG

Can you guess why this insect is called an earwig? People used to think that it would crawl into their ears when they were asleep.

Of course, the earwig doesn't want to crawl into your ear! Yuck!

But it does like to hide in dark places in the daytime. It can fit in the smallest places. You might find it hiding in a book, in a tiny crack.

Careful! Don't try to pick it up. See those pinchers on its tail? It might try to pinch you! Or it might spray you with a bad-smelling spray.

But don't blame the earwig. If you were that small, you would pinch, too.

In the night, the earwig creeps out of its hiding place. It looks for fruit or plants to eat. It will also eat your garbage for you.

Most insects don't take care of their babies. But the mother earwig does. She watches over her babies after they hatch. She doesn't want other insects to eat them. Her babies are glad that she has those sharp pinchers.

The Earwig's Complaint

Some folks must think I'm crazy!
I wish they'd just relax.
Why would I crawl in your stupid old ear?
Those things are full of *wax*!

37

CICADA

What is that rustling in the grass? What are all these creepy creatures crawling along the ground? They look like little tanks with red eyes. There are hundreds and hundreds of them.

It's like a whole insect army rolling along. What if they roll right over your toes? Will they chew them up?

Don't worry. A cicada can't bite. Its mouth is like a little straw. The only thing it can suck is plant juice.

The cicadas are in a hurry. For years and years they have lived under the ground. They snoozed in the dark. All they did was suck juice from roots. Weren't they bored down there?

All at once they decide to dig out. Now they are all crawling toward the nearest tree. They climb up the trunk and creep out of their old skins. You can find the skins still hanging on the tree trunks. They look like little suits of armor.

The cicada army climbs to the tops of the trees. The males start calling to the females. Their voices make a loud, ugly buzzing.

The females love the buzzing. It sounds like music to them. They search and search to find out who is making that nice song. Then they mate.

Afterwards, the female makes a slit in a twig. She lays her eggs in it. Then she dies.

Soon the babies hatch and fall to the ground. Quickly, they dig a tunnel to live in. Then they snuggle down in the dark for years and years.

Some kinds of cicadas stay underground for seventeen years. That's a long time to stay in bed!

A Cicada Lullaby

Go to bed, my little one,
And snooze all safe and sound.
Close your eyes
(There's nothing to see)
And drowse in the dark, underground.
I won't get you up in the morning,
There's no need to bother your head
With lessons, or dentists, or schooling–
You can spend your whole childhood in bed.

PRAYING MANTIS

What is this giant green monster? It has huge goggly eyes. Its mouth is like a pair of scissors. Its front legs open and close like a jackknife. There are hooks and spines all over its legs.

Will it try to eat you?

Yes! But only if you are an insect. The praying mantis will eat bugs and beetles and caterpillars. It will eat a hornet or a bee or a dragonfly. It will even try to eat a mouse or a snake. What if it can't find anything to eat? It will eat another praying mantis.

If a bird tries to eat it, it will fight back. It will even fight with a cat. But it will not bite people. Maybe it thinks people don't taste good.

Can you guess how it gets its name? All day long it sits very still in the grass, its front legs up in front of its face, like someone praying.

Maybe it's praying for an insect to come by. It snatches it up and holds it tight with its folding front legs. Then the praying mantis bites the insect's neck to kill it. In no time it gobbles up its dinner.

It can be hard to find a praying mantis, because it looks like the grass it sits on. But maybe you can find its egg case. Look in a field in the early spring. The egg case looks like a ball of old yellow sponge.

You can take the egg case home. Put it in a big jar and punch holes in the top for air. Put the jar in a sunny window.

One day hundreds of tiny babies will hatch. They look just like their giant mother. But they are small and cute.

Quick! Let them go outside. If you don't, they will eat each other up!

The Prayer of the Mantis

The mantis sits on a lettuce leaf
And prays to the Insect God:
"Send me some dinner, please,
Oh, please?
Is that so very hard?
Send me a beetle,
Send me a bug,
A soft one or a hard one.
I'll gobble it up from nose to tail
Before *it* eats the *garden!*"

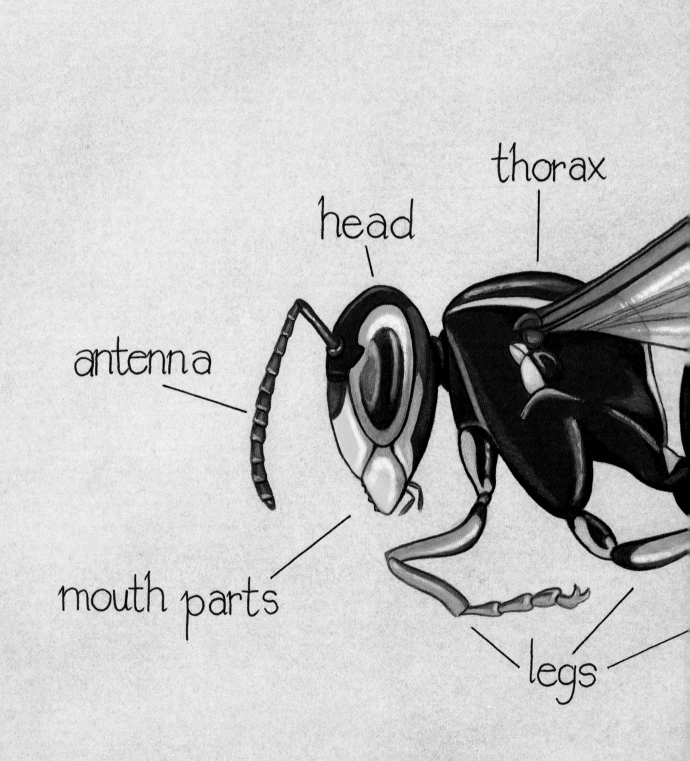

thorax

head

antenna

mouth parts

legs

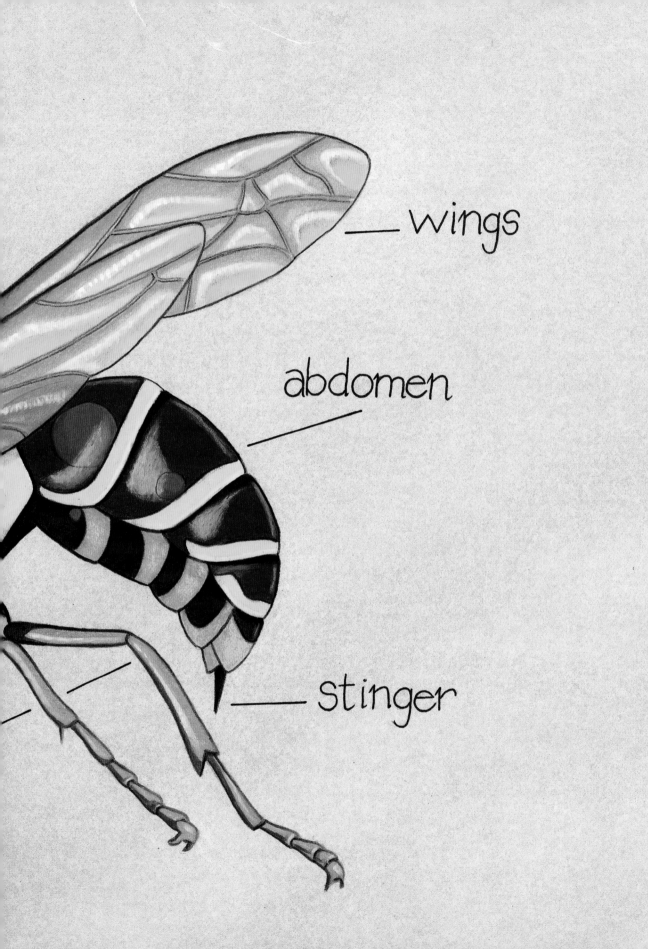

wings

abdomen

stinger

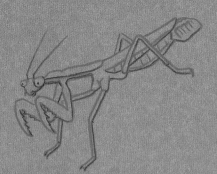

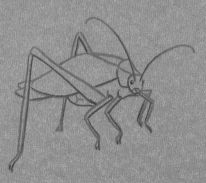

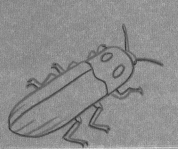
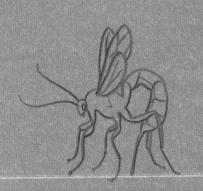